SAVING FRANKIE

Also by and with

Bobbi Phelps

Flyfishing Always

Writes of Passage 2011

Behind the Smile:
During the Glamour years of Aviation

Black Empress

For tray,
who loves cats~
Enjoy! Bobbi

SAVING FRANKIE

Adventures of a Rescued Barn Cat

Bobbi Phelps

Published in the United States by Village Concepts, L.L.C.
First Edition.

Creative Nonfiction Disclaimer: Recollections are to the best of my knowledge. To aid in the narrative flow, timelines have been condensed.

Cover layout and design by WC Publishing Services.
Illustrations by Anna Duong and Tracy Sprout.

Library of Congress Cataloging-in-Publication Data
1. Wolverton, Barbara Phelps. 2. Phelps, Bobbi. 3. Cat.
4. Illustrations. 5. Coloring Book. 6. Animal and Wildlife.
7. Author -- American. 8. Memoir. 9. Idaho. 10. Tennessee.

ISBN 978-0-9970688-2-5

eBook ISBN 978-0-9970688-3-2

Author's website at www.booksbybobbi.com.

Back cover: Photo of Bobbi and Frankie by Matt Wolverton.

In Memory
of
Frankie

my adventurous barn cat

CONTENTS:

Chapter One
Rescued

He hung by his front paws fifteen feet above the barn floor. The kitten had wrapped his body around the top rung of an old wooden ladder, screaming for all to hear. Scared to let go, but drained from the awkward position he held, he let out a wail that vibrated throughout the log barn.

About seven that morning, I had walked into the stable to give my horse his last carrot before returning to my home in central Idaho. The dark interior, lit only by the soft rays of the early sun, had formed dancing shadows along the shaded stall walls. Out of the corner of my eye, I noticed slight movements coming from high in the loft above my head.

Suddenly, I heard a shriek that startled me, and caused me to jump. It sounded like a wounded animal.

"Help me! Save me!" the creature seemed to be screaming.

Looking up, I noticed a tiny ball of white fur squirming at the top of the ladder. I ran to its edge and climbed up, extending my hands to unwind the crying kitten from the upper rung. With his body cradled in my arms and firmly held against my body, I climbed higher and found the mama cat, gently settling him next to his seven siblings.

The squirming kittens were nestled in a swirl of golden straw that had been scattered throughout the high loft. The grey mama cat curled herself among the tiny babies and let them nurse from her ample belly. I watched for a few minutes, surprised to see the kittens had a variety of colors and hair lengths.

Standing on the ladder inspecting the mama and her kittens, I recalled the purpose for my being in the barn. A few months earlier, my sister had telephoned to ask me to join her at a dude ranch. Ginny who lived in Pennsylvania,

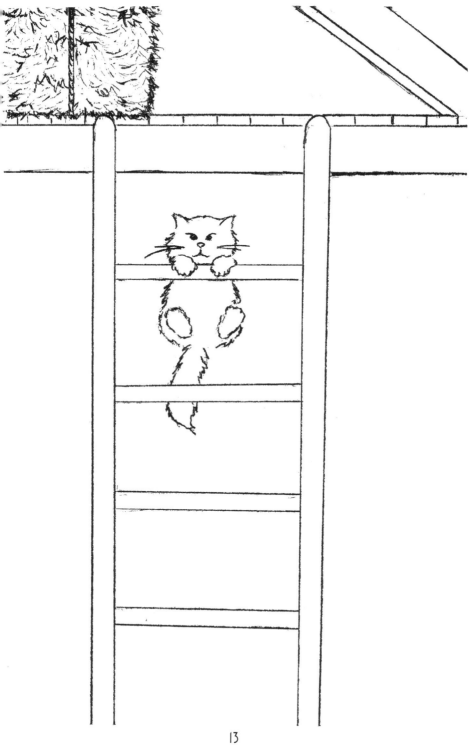

PLEASE COLOR THE DRAWING ON THE REVERSE SIDE
AND
ADD YOUR NAME AND DATE TO THIS PAGE

Name: _____ Date: _____

wrote for *Horse Illustrated Magazine* and would be on assignment not far from my Idaho home.

"We'll do simple chores and ride horses all day," she said. "You'll pay the owner for the privilege of staying in his bunkhouse and eating his meals," she added with a smile in her voice.

"Sure, I'd love to go. The ranch is only a few hours from here, so come stay with us before your assignment begins."

Once Ginny's plans were known, I asked Vickie, a friend and former Miss Rodeo Idaho, to tag along. The three of us, all young women starting out in life, would partner for a few days working a cattle ranch in eastern Idaho.

"I'll drive," said Vickie, a beautiful blond who lived on a small farm outside the capital city of Boise. "Since I'm bringing my own horse, we might as well go in my truck."

And so we did. Wearing faded blue jeans and work shirts, we traveled east from my home near Twin Falls to meet the owners of a large cattle operation, located a good three hours away.

Inside the main ranch house that night, we sat around a large oak table and ate with Mr.

Harris and his family. The smell of beef stew filled the kitchen as we bowed our heads in prayer before the meal.

"We'll gather for breakfast at six tomorrow morning," he instructed. "You'll begin your chores right after."

As participants at the dude ranch, we rode trusty cow ponies on steep mountainsides and found stubborn cattle that had wandered away from the main herd. We struggled as we moved the cows to greener pastures several miles away. In the increasing warmth of the day's sun, we worked long hours up and down the nearby mountains. It was fun, exhilarating, and exhausting.

Back in the bunkhouse that evening, the three of us laughed at the rancher's unique way of making money while ensuring his chores were accomplished. Before long, we had completed four days of hard labor while paying the dude rancher for the privilege of doing so. It was in Mr. Harris' barn that I had found the dangling kitten high on the ladder.

Most barn cats do not have the luxury of vaccinations, as veterinarian expenses are usually out of the question. Barn cats live off rodents and birds; consequently, they suffer from many diseases.

Knowing that the kitten's future would be brief and harsh, I asked the muscular rancher if I could take the baby cat home.

"Of course," he said. "I have plenty more." And he gave me an old shoebox to transport the six-week-old cat.

A shrill meow often interrupted our long drive home. The kitten seemed to be saying, "Where's my mama? Where's my family?"

In the backseat, Ginny removed the kitten from the shoebox and lifted him up for us to see. The fluff of fur was not much to look at—part Siamese and part long-hair tabby. He was totally white except for an orange nose and orange-tipped ears. He had bright blue eyes that reminded us of our parents' favorite singer, Frank Sinatra, better known as "old blue eyes." So we named him Frankie.

By the time we arrived home, Frankie had settled down and cried only a couple of times. Warm milk and kitten kibbles satisfied his hunger and my petting satisfied his trust. It didn't take him long to bond with me and for me to bond with him. We began a life-long love and affection for each other on that very day.

Because Frankie was part Siamese, his eyes crossed and he had poor depth perception. I soon discovered that his jumping ability lacked a cat's ordinary skills and contributed to his many awkward landings.

He often soared from the cement steps that jutted from the kitchen door to the garage interior, alighting on a metal counter nearby. I kept his kitten kibble in a bowl on top of the counter, high off the floor so our family dog would not take advantage of the easy chow.

Most of the time Frankie made precise jumps, but periodically he leaped into the air and landed a few inches to the side of the four-foot-high cabinet. After he fell to the garage floor, he typically shook his head in stunned surprise.

"What happened?" he seemed to ask.

About a year after his rescue, Frankie decided to jump from the top of our gas grill to a low-hanging portion of the house roof, a little above the outdoor patio. He shot straight up and missed the roof by a solid foot.

Frankie flew into the lower window, plastering himself against the glass, his arms and legs stretched in all directions. I watched him slide down the five-foot, vertical window to the bricks below, reminding me of Garfield, the comic-strip cat.

Upon landing, he shook his head in surprise. Again, he appeared to wonder, "What just happened?"

Chapter Two
Hiding

Summer in the Rocky Mountains meant time for fishing and camping. My young son, Matt, and I loaded our tan truck and added last-minute gear and food. The drive to our favorite lake would take five hours, and I knew we would be snacking along the way. Extra sodas had been packed in the oversized cooler in the middle of the truckbed.

Since the camping trip would last only a few days, Matt had left plenty of food and water for Frankie on the tool cabinet in the garage. He could easily survive in the large, cavernous area for the long weekend. He had his litter box, food, water, and plenty of spots to explore once I pulled down the folding, attic stairs. Frankie, now three years old, was a happy and enthusiastic cat — always wanting to investigate new regions and possibly find a mouse or two in the process.

After all our supplies had been packed, Matt and I piled inside the pickup for the long drive to the lake. As we maneuvered out the driveway, we realized that our sodas would be hard to reach in the middle of our truck.

"Let's go back," Matt suggested. "It'll be easier to get drinks from the fridge now than later on."

I drove back to our house, exited the truck, and unlocked the back door. Walking into the empty garage, I looked around to see if anything had been left behind. Not noticing Frankie, I assumed he had already climbed the ladder and had now begun to search the attic.

With a bag in my left hand, I reached for the handle of the spare refrigerator in the garage and opened the door. Out sprang Frankie! Flying past me, he escaped from the cold interior, a blur of white fluff racing beside my legs.

PLEASE COLOR THE DRAWING ON THE REVERSE SIDE
AND
ADD YOUR NAME AND DATE TO THIS PAGE

Name: _____ Date: _____

Somehow he had sneaked into the white refrigerator while we had packed the cooler with food and sodas, accidentally leaving the door ajar. We hadn't noticed — his white fur blended in perfectly. Thank goodness I had decided to retrieve the sodas. We would have returned three days later to a very cold and, possibly, a very dead cat.

From then on, I always looked for places that Frankie might hide: in deep closets, under beds, in boxes, in suitcases, or behind recliners. Any secluded dark corner would become a favorite hiding place. I tried to confirm his whereabouts each evening, verifying that he was still inside. He was such an escape artist. After checking the house and finding Frankie, I could then relax and go to bed.

Chapter Three
Mice and Fights

A chorus of birds awakened me at dawn several years later. I rolled over to listen to their early morning chirps and slowly climbed out of bed. After pausing a few minutes, I dressed and sleepily walked to the kitchen to have some toast and orange juice.

When I opened the door to the garage, there stood Frankie clutching a live rodent in his mouth. Looking very pleased with himself, he struggled to bring the squirming object inside.

"No way!" I shouted and pushed him back from the door with my bare foot.

Immediately, Frankie dropped the thrashing mouse. The grey bundle raced over my toes and darted into the kitchen. Frankie chased after him, and I ran to the closet to retrieve a broom.

With much spinning and sweeping, I managed to brush the mouse out of the house, but not fast enough. Frankie was in fierce pursuit right behind him. He grabbed the speeding rodent and ran into a nearby pasture, disappearing into a harvested field. Now fully awake, I cradled my glass of juice and began to dress for work.

That afternoon a grey mouse tail lay on the cement steps by my back door, the remains of the morning gift. As a topnotch predator, Frankie provided me with a smorgasbord of animal parts on an almost daily basis.

However, while he inspected the fields and neighborhood, he frequently fought with local cats. They defeated him every time. He returned home with ripped ears, neck bites, and numerous punctures. Chunks of white silky hair informed my neighbors, Ginger and Dexter Rogers, that Frankie had been in their fenced yard and had lost another battle to their feisty black cat.

.

PLEASE COLOR THE DRAWING ON THE REVERSE SIDE
AND
ADD YOUR NAME AND DATE TO THIS PAGE

Name: _____ Date: _____

At the local veterinarian's office, I noticed Frankie's bills had skyrocketed from the results of his fights. Much to his displeasure, he became an indoor cat. Consequently, any time someone accidentally left my house door ajar, he rushed outside and escaped to mouse heaven.

Frankie might have been a loser of battles outside, but inside he ruled the roost. Living by myself after a divorce, and with Matt now away at college, I became dependent on my friends and animals for company. A large dog named Casey, a black tabby named Zipper, and Frankie were my constant companions. Everywhere I went in my home, they followed, with Frankie leading the parade.

My routine in the evening was to take a bath before climbing into bed. This became my personal quiet time. On one particular night, I lay in a bubble-filled tub and pulled the shower curtain closed, giving me absolute privacy. Casey and Frankie sat on the bath mat, waiting patiently for me to finish bathing. Meanwhile, black-haired Zipper walked along the wide edge of the tub, on the inside of the transparent drape.

As I soaked calmly in the warm water, truly at peace, Frankie noticed a dark shadow moving on the inside of the curtain. He pounced. Frankie smashed Zipper into the bath water, right onto my chest. Thinking she was going to drown, the wet cat scrambled from the tub, racing cross my body and flying over my face.

"Get out!" I screamed and stood straight up, dripping in trickles of blood and bubbles.

All three animals raced from my fury. I slammed the bathroom door behind them as tails disappeared into the house interior. The serenity of the bath, however, had now vanished.

Chapter Four
Blinded

On a beautiful autumn morning, wisps of sunlight crept across the garage floor, settling on the metal tool cabinet. I had been packing boxes, moving furniture, and eliminating extra supplies. In a few months I planned to leave Idaho and drive cross-country to Tennessee.

Many years had passed since I had rescued that tiny kitten in the old barn in the foothills of Idaho. Casey and Zipper had since surrendered to old age and died. Frankie was now my only pet.

While moving about the house, Frankie, anxious and uneasy, followed me everywhere. Soon he began to meow, telling me five o'clock had arrived, and he wanted his dinner. I left my chores and walked into the garage.

On the lid of the metal tool chest sat his food bowl, and inside the drawers lay cans of cat meat and tuna fish. Just as I opened a drawer to remove a can, Frankie jumped into the air, attempting to land on top of the four-foot-high cabinet. He missed his target.

His body collided with the steel chest and his eye hit the sharp metal corner of the drawer. I watched in horror as he screamed loudly and fell to the floor, his eye bulging from the crash. Cradling him in my arms, I inspected his injury. It looked awful.

I placed Frankie in his cat carrier and quickly drove to my veterinarian's office. After the doctor examined his eye, he confirmed my suspicions. Frankie was now completely blind in the damaged eye.

Back at home I held Frankie, fussing over him, and stroking his furry back. He nuzzled his nose next to mine, purred, and then nestled into my lap. In spite of his many worrisome adventures, he seemed to be a happy cat and continued to be content.

At the end of the month, my neighbors, Ginger and Dexter, were invited for dinner. They had been wonderful friends for many years, and I wanted to share one last meal with them before packing my pots, dishes, and cooking utensils.

From the small kitchen, I could see into the living room as I prepared the salad. I heard Frankie batting a tiny ball of paper around the vinyl floor — pouncing on it and tossing it high into the air.

Not being much of a cook, I became engrossed in the meal preparation, anxious to make a special dinner. I never noticed the sudden silence.

Before long, strange smells filled my nostrils. A cloud of sour smoke blew into the kitchen. There on the glass coffee table in front of the sofa lay Frankie, peacefully relaxing. As he rested, he raised and lowered his white tail over three short, burning candles. He had no notion of the nearby fire.

Cat hair does not burst into flames; it sizzles, smells, and turns black. Rushing to rescue Frankie from his impending incineration, I grabbed the napping cat. I placed him in the kitchen sink and ran cool water over his blackened tail.

Surprised from his sleep, he tried to flee and fought to escape. As I poured more water over his once-white tail, huge globs of blackened fur fell into the sink. The horrid smell was bitter and intense. Just then Ginger and Dexter walked in.

"What smells? Is that our dinner?" Ginger asked.

"No, it's not!" I answered indignantly. "Come here. Look what happened to Frankie!"

On the kitchen counter sat a wet cat with white hair sticking out from most of his body. He looked like he had had an electric shock. His long tail looked practically nude but for a small white, marshmallow-shaped tuft at the very end. I patted Frankie with a towel, rubbing and drying him. Before long he began to purr with pleasure while I carried him through the house, opening windows and turning on fans.

PLEASE COLOR THE DRAWING ON THE REVERSE SIDE
AND
ADD YOUR NAME AND DATE TO THIS PAGE

Name: _____ Date: _____

Frankie delighted in seeing my neighbors and quickly forgot his latest emergency. Soon the burnt-hair smell diminished, and I served a delicious dinner. The rest of the evening was uneventful. Laughter and stories of Frankie filled the room as we consumed the tasty stroganoff that I had just made.

Bobbi Phelps

Chapter Five
Moving

The moving van pulled into my driveway on a cool mountain morning. Packed boxes filled the garage, and suitcases stuffed my little car.

Muscular men, Craig and Jack, began removing the boxes from the garage and loading them onto their commercial van. Wanting to keep Frankie, my now ten-year-old rescue cat, protected from the chaos of the day's activities, I isolated him in my bedroom closet. He had a knack for escaping, and I wanted to keep him safe.

After many hours the large moving truck, crammed full and now out of sight, began its journey to Tennessee. Checking for missed items, I walked through the empty house. Eventually, I came to my bedroom and opened the door to the walk-in closet. It was empty!

"Where's Frankie?" I asked out loud.

I frantically searched everywhere, inspecting every cabinet and closet. Nothing! Where did Frankie go? Before long, the uniformed movers returned to my front door.

It seems Craig had opened my bedroom closet door hours earlier to verify that everything had been placed in the van. Apparently, Frankie took off, ran through the house, and climbed into the truck. No one had spotted the fleeing cat.

When they had driven five miles down the road, Jack decided to double-check the truck's contents before beginning the ten-day journey to Tennessee. And thank goodness he did!

They stopped on a nearby side road, surrounded by harvested corn fields, gold brush land, and rows of trees marking a farmer's fence lines. Jack opened one of the metal doors at the rear of the huge truck. As he eased the door to the side, a white blob flew over his shoulder and dashed from the dark enclosure into an adjacent pasture.

PLEASE COLOR THE DRAWING ON THE REVERSE SIDE
AND
ADD YOUR NAME AND DATE TO THIS PAGE

Name: _____ Date: _____

Frankie stopped to gather his bearings as soon as he reached the field. He loved people and when Jack called, "Kitty, kitty, kitty," Frankie allowed Jack to approach and pick him up.

When they returned to the house, I clasped Frankie in my arms and thanked the men for returning him to me. Immediately I enclosed him in his carrier and packed the few remaining items into my tiny car. Larry, my fiancé, had just arrived. He would drive us cross-country to our new home in Tennessee.

As we maneuvered through the farmland to the interstate, we heard persistent howling from the cat container in the backseat. Frankie was informing us that this adventure was not at all to his liking. After an hour of angry protests and constant crying, I placed him on my lap, and Larry continued to drive. Frankie now became a content, happy, and purring cat. But not for long.

He wanted to explore the car and soared from my lap, over our bodies to the luggage in the backseat. Because his claws had never been removed, Larry and I received serious scratch marks on our arms and shoulders as Frankie flew into the back seat.

That evening, we booked a room at an animal-friendly hotel near the highway. Larry placed Frankie's litter box in the bathroom and his food and water containers in the bedroom. Once everything was to Frankie's satisfaction, he joined us on the bed and we soon fell asleep.

Early the next morning, I decided to clean the litter box before Larry and I departed for breakfast. Knowing that litter can clog a toilet, I took only two soaked litter pieces, each about the size of a ping-pong ball, and placed them in the commode. Once I flushed the toilet, we walked to the dining room.

On our return, Larry and I discovered that the toilet had overflowed. Water spilled from the bathroom and into the bedroom, soaking the carpet, our books, maps, and everything else left on the floor.

I couldn't believe all the water. Even though I had only dropped a couple of small litter balls into the toilet, the pipes became totally blocked.

After notifying the hotel of the damage, the innkeeper responded, "No problem. We'll have it cleaned. And we'll keep your pet deposit."

Chapter Six
Lakeside

Autumn leaves covered the driveway and a slight chill filled the air. The moving men had now delivered our many possessions to the new lakeside home we had just purchased. After they left and all the cardboard boxes were deposited in specific rooms, Larry and I began unpacking. Frankie explored his new surroundings, amazed by an open door to a fenced deck on the second floor.

"What was that?" Larry asked as he sat at his desk, putting away pencils and pens in the top drawer.

The large windows of his ground-floor office faced the lake. He saw a flash of white fall down in front of him. It looked like a pillow had been dropped from the deck above.

When Larry walked out the back door, he saw Frankie standing on a patch of grass twelve feet below the deck railing. Frankie wobbled forward, stunned from the fall. Because he had one blind eye and one cross eye, he lacked depth perception. He had looked between the fence rails, but had never realized how far the drop to the ground would be. Larry gently picked him up, stroked his back, and brought him inside.

During the upcoming year, Frankie went over the railing three more times. The worst event occurred when I awoke after midnight to discover he was no longer in the house. I had forgotten to check his whereabouts before going to sleep.

I noticed large black clouds passing in front of the moon and searched the house and outside kitchen deck. Nothing. No Frankie anywhere. Far out on the skyline, a storm was gathering. A flash of lightening lit the lake, immediately followed by a thunderclap.

I closed the front door behind me and walked in my pajamas to the busy road in front of our house. I made my way slowly, the wind whipping my bathrobe around me.

"Frankie! Frankie!" I called, but he couldn't be found.

As the gusts lashed at me, I again went to the kitchen deck and called his name. Immediately, I heard a shrill meow coming from under our neighbor's flowering shrub.

I raced downstairs, out the back door, and grabbed Frankie, gently fussing over him as I brought him inside. Another bolt of lightning split the darkness.

Within five minutes the clouds opened up, and intense rain battered against the windows. Our twenty-year-old home suffered one of the worst drenches it had ever experienced. From that night on, Frankie never jumped over the railing, and I never went to bed without double-checking his whereabouts.

These episodes were not the only issues we had with our adventurous cat. One summer evening, when Larry traveled out of town, Frankie and I followed the path to our small dock that extended into the lake. I sat on a cushioned chair at the very end of the dock and gathered Frankie into my lap. We watched the sun's rays sink below the horizon as I rubbed his silky fur.

As the sun lost its strength, and it became darker and cooler, I said, "OK, Frankie. Let's go inside."

Frankie jumped from my lap and walked toward the house. He waited at the rope railing surrounding our dock and looked up.

All of a sudden he leaped unto the wide brown rope. It paused for a nanosecond. Then it reacted to his surge and flung him into the lake.

Frankie immediately dropped below the surface and disappeared. Small sheets of water splashed from where he had landed. I could see nothing but black water. Then his head emerged, his blue eyes wide with fright. He paddled like mad, but he was too far for me to reach.

Finally, he turned and flicked his tail toward me. I grasped the white extremity and pulled him closer. Grabbing his body, I lifted him from the lake and cradled him in my arms, soaking my blouse and shorts.

PLEASE COLOR THE DRAWING ON THE REVERSE SIDE
AND
ADD YOUR NAME AND DATE TO THIS PAGE

Name: _____ Date: _____

Before long I had Frankie inside our house, wrapped in a towel and rubbed dry. Coming from Idaho, he had never seen outside water. We had lived in a desert-like area that received only eight inches of rain a year. His first experience created quite an impression, one that he surely never wanted to suffer again.

Chapter Seven
Christmas

"What's that?" my neighbor Carol shouted as she jumped back from our Christmas tree. "Is that Frankie?"

Frankie had climbed over the brass bucket at the tree's base and sneaked up the artificial trunk until he found a level branch. He perched close to the shaft and peered out, right at eye height.

"He scared me to death! What's he doing?" Carol exclaimed.

"Just checking on us," I answered. "He loves the crinkle of wrapping paper and the surprises he finds in holiday boxes and bags. Christmas is his favorite time of the year and watching us from the tree is what he does. He's been climbing our tree for fifteen years, ever since he was a kitten."

"Don't the ornaments get knocked off? How about the tree? Can he tip it over?" Carol asked.

"No, the tree is fine — and so are the ornaments," I said. "However, the miniature carolers have fallen a few times. He likes to leap from the back of Larry's armchair to the fireplace mantel," I added, pointing to a few decorative carolers placed on the wood shelf above the hearth.

"He even climbs onto the wreath above the fireplace and actually sleeps in the sway of the circle, right between the decorative gold stars and ivy. It's amazing."

Just then our outside lights on the kitchen deck illuminated snowflakes falling in a flurry. Carol said she had to go. She zipped up her jacket,

PLEASE COLOR THE DRAWING ON THE REVERSE SIDE
AND
ADD YOUR NAME AND DATE TO THIS PAGE

Name: _____ Date: _____

added boots, and left to walk the short distance home. Within minutes she had disappeared into the darkness.

Larry and I had now lived in Tennessee for five years and Frankie had settled in —learning to live as an indoor cat, but always trying to duplicate his previous outdoor life.

When we went to bed that night, Frankie took his normal place on Larry's chest. Soon Larry fell asleep, and Frankie moved to my half of the bed. Once I turned out the light and rolled over to sleep on my stomach, he curled up, leaning against my side.

As the evening wore on, I became unusually hot. Whipping the heavy blanket from my body, I accidentally tossed a sleeping Frankie three feet into the air. He flew across the room and bounced over the footboard at the end of our sleigh bed. He crashed on the other side, creating a deep thumping noise.

I flicked on the bedside light and rushed to his side. Frankie stood on his feet, groggy and shaking his head, wondering what had just happened. Taking him in my arms, I returned to the bed and placed him on my chest, stroking his smooth fur.

The next day, Larry and I removed the footboard and listed our bed on Craig's list. No way did we want Frankie to endure another flying episode.

After a couple of weeks, my son, Matt, and his dog came to visit for the holidays. Pete, an American bulldog, weighed seventy pounds and was about the size of a boxer with the brown, black, and white markings of an English bulldog.

He came bounding into the house and spied Frankie on a nearby chair. Typical of dogs discovering other animals, he went directly over to sniff the cat.

Frankie reacted immediately. Hissing, he slapped Pete right across his face. With an arched back and hair standing straight up, Frankie continued to hiss.

Never having met a cat before, Pete recoiled from the sharp claws flying across his face. Bleeding from his nose, he ran behind

Matt, cowering from our spitting cat. Our little Frankie was now the boss; he had proved his dominance. We no longer had to worry about their size differences.

Over the weeklong visit, Pete avoided Frankie at all times. He refused to cross any threshold if our cat lounged by the door. He also would not go anywhere near our cat, whether at dinner time or not. Consequently, Frankie took advantage of his power and purposely stretched out in doorways, hallways, and even on Pete's doggy bed. Inciting Frankie was not in Pete's makeup and, in our house, that was never going to happen.

Chapter Eight
The Red Chair

"Hey, Mom. Can you watch Pete for a year?" my son asked over the phone.

"What do you mean, a year?" I questioned. Although we had looked after his American bulldog a few months earlier, it had only been for a week.

"The Coast Guard has assigned me overseas to an island in the Persian Gulf," Matt answered. "I'll be heading out shortly. What'd you think?"

"Of course, it's all right. We'll pick him up whenever you're ready."

Larry and I enjoyed having Pete in our home; he was perfect — easygoing and friendly. We retrieved him a few weeks later.

On our return from North Carolina where Matt had been stationed, Larry glanced in the rearview mirror and saw Pete leaning over the back seat, checking his belongings. We were bringing his toys, food, towels, and a crate to his new and temporary home.

"We'll have a great time with him. I've always wanted a big dog," Larry said.

When we arrived at our townhouse, we reintroduced Pete to Frankie. We had no need to be concerned about their size differences. Pete remembered Frankie very well from his earlier visit. Pete kept his distance from our aging cat at all times.

Later that first evening, Larry went to bed while I completed a jigsaw puzzle. Frankie curled up on our couch, blending his white body into the cushion folds while Pete rested on a soft carpet many feet away from our sleeping cat. Orange embers from the log fire lit one end of the living room and the smell of pine needles scented the air. Everything seemed so quiet and peaceful.

An hour or so later, I closed the fireplace door and retired to our bedroom. While I read propped against a pillow, Frankie climbed into my lap and nestled among the layers of my pajamas, drifting off to sleep. He closed his eyes and purred when I rubbed behind his ears and around his collar.

At the arched doorway to our bedroom, Pete breathed deeply, composing himself as he advanced into the room. He knew that Frankie was nearby. Within minutes, however, he fell asleep, curled into his favorite red comfy chair next to my side of the bed. The arms of the recliner wrapped around the sleeping dog. Pete and Larry made gentle snoring sounds as I turned the pages of a mystery book.

While I read, Frankie left my lap and climbed over the adjacent nightstand. Maybe Pete was sleeping too close to me or maybe Frankie had to prove his dominance. Who knows what a cat thinks?

Frankie slinked his way toward Pete and stretched until his front paws lay on the arm of the red recliner. With hisses just inches from the sleeping dog's body, Frankie continued to creep forward. Pete did not move. He was sound asleep, dead to the world.

I decided that Frankie had annoyed Pete enough and reached over, firmly pulling back on the cat's tail. When I yanked his tail, Frankie must have thought something had attacked him. He let out a piercing scream, right beside Pete's ear.

Pete awakened from his deep sleep. He looked up and saw our white cat hovering just above him. His eyes widened and he exploded from the red chair. With terrified barks and loud shrieks, they both bolted from the room.

"What happened?" Larry shouted as he sat straight up in bed.

I laughed so hard, tears streamed down my face. I couldn't answer. Soon Larry was back to sleep, and I began to ponder the presumed peacefulness of our next twelve months with Pete and Frankie.

PLEASE COLOR THE DRAWING ON THE REVERSE SIDE
AND
ADD YOUR NAME AND DATE TO THIS PAGE

Name: _____ Date: _____

Chapter Nine
The Ninth Life

Frankie and Pete survived a chaotic year together. The first few months exposed Frankie as a small, intimidating cat over a large, muscular dog. The last three months ended with a peaceful truce.

When I called them for dinner, they raced to their assigned spots. At nighttime, Pete darted to the bedroom with Frankie right behind him. They both enjoyed the deck extending from our kitchen and finally accepted each other's presence while relaxing in the outdoor space.

Once Matt had completed his Coast Guard assignment, Pete returned with him to their home in the Carolinas. Larry, Frankie, and I were back to normal — or so we thought.

"Have you noticed a difference in Frankie?" I asked Larry. "He doesn't come anymore. Watch."

I stood about five feet from Frankie and called his name. Usually, he would perk up and come right to me. Now he did nothing. He just lay there, ignoring me.

"Do you think he's deaf?" Larry asked.

"I never thought of that. I'll check the internet."

Sure enough, Frankie was indeed deaf. And he probably had been during part of the year we watched Pete. When I queried *deaf cats*, the internet informed me that, although deaf cats can't hear, they can feel vibrations. Whenever I had called both animals, Frankie must have responded to the big dog's pounding feet.

During the first night without Pete, with just the three of us, Frankie left our bedroom to feed and use his litter box. When he returned at about two in the morning, he had no idea where we were. He couldn't see us sleeping under the quilted covers.

He lifted his voice in a wild shriek, standing under the arch of our bedroom door. It was a roaring wail that came deep from within his

PLEASE COLOR THE DRAWING ON THE REVERSE SIDE
AND
ADD YOUR NAME AND DATE TO THIS PAGE

Name: _____ Date: _____

chest. The screeching sound bounced off the walls and seemed as loud as could be.

Frankie drew in another deep breath. As the air rushed out of him, it carried a long scream. The hair on the back of my neck stood up, and Larry and I sat straight up in bed. We turned on the lights and looked around. Once Frankie saw us, he stopped screaming and jumped onto the bed, curling into his favorite spot.

For the next sixteen months a screaming cat prevailed. Whenever Frankie could not see us, he would begin to wail. He never wanted to be left alone and became anxious and confused. We learned to clap our hands or stamp our feet so Frankie would know where to find us.

Toward the end of May, I noticed that Frankie walked carefully down our carpeted stairs, not bouncing as he normally did. And for a beautiful white cat, his grooming had now stopped. He seemed to lack his usual energy, eating very little, and sleeping long hours in a dark spot under a corner table.

One day Frankie jumped off our bed and fell, hurting his right front leg. He floundered to lick his sore foot, twisted and fell again. Tears brimmed in my eyes. I picked him up, shocked to feel even more bones beneath his skin.

He tried to rub his head against my chin and even struggled to purr. When I put him down, he bumped into the dresser as he wobbled toward the door, fell again, and staggered forward.

Frankie was deaf, had lost his appetite, and was becoming totally blind. I didn't want to admit the inevitable. After seventeen years together, it became too hard for me to believe. I finally surrendered.

"Larry, I think Frankie's dying," I sobbed. Larry sadly agreed and reluctantly called the veterinarian's office to make one last appointment.

When we arrived at the animal hospital, we were tenderly ushered into a private side room. I dropped the towel that wrapped Frankie and held him to my chest. Larry put his arms around both of us, and we wept as we waited.

"We love you, Frankie. It'll soon be over," I whispered.

Tears streamed down our faces when the veterinarian appeared. He calmly talked to us and shaved Frankie's front leg. As he spoke, the doctor inserted a sharp needle into Frankie's leg. Almost immediately, our loving cat sank to the stainless-steel table.

After listening to his heart slow and then stop, the doctor said, "Frankie's gone."

Larry and I sobbed out loud. We were heartbroken. Frankie had helped me through a divorce, he had welcomed Larry to our household, and he had brought laughter and stories to our family and friends. We took him home, wrapped in his favorite towel, and buried him under a large stone near our flower garden.

EPILOGUE:

July 9 was a sad day — an end to our beloved and adventurous barn cat named Frankie.

Days went by and Larry and I couldn't seem to get over the loss. Frankie's death was unfair and we hurt from his absence, but life went on.

Our clouds eventually turned to sunshine. We visited with friends and began to laugh again. We, once more, focused on the beauty of life, to remember the good times with Frankie, and to know that he was in a better place with no more pain.

Rescuing Frankie brought us much happiness and many rewards. He lived a full life and added excitement and sparkle to ours. So many stories and so much fun for us to have Frankie for seventeen years.

ACKNOWLEDGEMENTS

I am indebted to all those who have encouraged and helped me through my years of writing. It's from their words of support that I have been able to continue my work. A special thanks from me to my sister, Ginny Clemens; my golfing buddies Ginny Cortright, Carol Moehrke, and Sue Woodrup; Idaho friends Nancy and Doug Strand, Ginger and Dexter Rogers; my son, Matt Wolverton; and the love of my life, Larry Chapman.

Cover Design: WC Publishing Services, Stevens Point, Wisconsin.

Editing: Jody Amato at jodyamato@gmail.com, and Kathy Economy at kathyeconomy@gmail.com.

Formatting: WC Publishing Services, Stevens Point, Wisconsin.

Illustrations: Anna Duong and Tracy Sprout at sprout.myrandf@gmail.com.

Web Page: Abraham Tol at abrahamtol@atol-solutions.com.

ABOUT THE AUTHOR

Photo by
Cinthia D. Stafford

Bobbi Phelps grew up in Connecticut, forty miles from New York City. Following graduation from Pine Manor College, she joined the airline industry as an international flight attendant.

In 1967 Bobbi traveled solo around the world and returned to complete her education at the University of California, Berkeley.

She began writing books in 2011 and has completed five to date with three more to be published in the next few years: *Home on the Range* in 2018; *Growing up in the Forties and Fifties* in 2019; and *Hitchhiking Africa, the British Isles, and New Zealand* in 2020. Her fiancé, Larry Chapman, has helped throughout the process by fixing her computer, running errands, and escorting her to numerous speaking engagements.

About the Author:

- Arnold Gingrich Writers Award from the International Federation of Fly Fishers.

- Twenty-year member of the Outdoor Writers Association of America.

- President of the Authors Guild of Tennessee.

- Member of the Knoxville Writers Group.

- Writes periodic travel series for The Connection in Lenoir City, Tennessee.

- Created the Angler's Calendar Company and won Exporter of the Year for the State of Idaho.

- Nine-year Idaho board member of The Nature Conservancy.

Bobbi enjoys hearing from her readers. Visit her website. She'll respond directly.

Happy Reading!

www.booksbybobbi.com

Saving Frankie
An Adventurous Rescue Barn Cat

by

BOBBI PHELPS

$_____ $14.95 times _____ number of signed copies.
$_____ 9% Tax ($1.35 each book if mailed to Tennessee).
$_____ U.S.A. Shipping & Handling. ($2.99 each book).

$_____ **Total** ($17.94 each book w/o tax). Ck # _____
              Make check out to Village Concepts.

Email: _____

Visa/ MC #: _____

Expiration: _____ 3-Digit Code: _____

Mailing address:
    Street: _____

    City: _____

    State: _____ Zip: _____

Contact for multiple order discount.

www.booksbybobbi.com

Village Concepts, LLC, 124 Chota Shores, Loudon TN 37774.

BEHIND THE SMILE

During the Glamour Years of Aviation
"A Flight Attendant's Journey"

by

BOBBI PHELPS WOLVERTON

$_____ $14.95 times _____ number of signed copies.
$_____ 9% Tax ($1.35 each book if mailed to Tennessee).
$_____ U.S.A. Shipping & Handling. ($2.99 each book).

$_____ Total ($17.94 each book w/o tax). Ck # _____
    Make check out to Village Concepts.

Email: _____

Visa/ MC #: _____

Expiration: _____ 3-Digit Code: _____

Mailing address:
    Street: _____

    City: _____

    State: _____ Zip: _____

Contact for multiple order discount.

www.booksbybobbi.com

Village Concepts, LLC, 124 Chota Shores, Loudon TN 37774.

BLACK EMPRESS

Rescuing a Puppy from Iran

by

BOBBI PHELPS WOLVERTON

$_____ $14.95 times _____ number of signed copies.
$_____ 9% Tax ($1.35 each book if mailed to Tennessee).
$_____ U.S.A. Shipping & Handling. ($2.99 each book).

$_____ **Total** ($17.94 each book w/o tax). Ck # _____
Make check out to Village Concepts.

Email: _____

Visa/ MC #: _____

Expiration: _____ 3-Digit Code: _____

Mailing address:
　　Street: _____

　　City: _____

　　State: _____ Zip: _____

Contact for multiple order discount.

www.booksbybobbi.com

Village Concepts, LLC, 124 Chota Shores, Loudon TN 37774.

REVIEWS:

Andrea J. Cys, Age 13: "Frankie seemed like a wonderful and adventurous cat! I wish I had the chance to meet him! Overall, the book was captivating and funny, and I really enjoyed it and would eminently recommend it to others."

Ansley Wassell, Age 12: "Frankie was a very sweet and tender cat. I loved reading about his adventures...especially the one about the moving van."

Becker Andrews, Age 11: I hope other kids will enjoy this book as much as I did. It keeps you laughing at Frankie's antics."

Emma Dorsey, Age 10: "I loved the book! I loved Frankie! It's a wonderful story about a wonderful cat!"

Sam Wassell, Age 13: "I enjoyed reading about Frankie's adventures, especially the one about the time he got trapped inside the fridge. Frankie was a funny cat because he always wanted to be with people."

Tinsley Andrews, Age 9: "Frankie was an adventurous and curious cat that enjoyed all of his nine lives just like I did when I read his stories. You should read this book!"